SONATINA | *Masterworks*

series of DYNAMIC *and* VIBRANT *sonatinas*

for performers of all ages

This book is dedicated to Ashley Magrath

Cover art: Interior of Saint Peter's, Rome (1735)
by Giovanni Paolo Pannini (Italian, 1691–1765)
Oil on canvas (60 1/4" x 86 1/2")
The Norton Simon Foundation, Pasadena, California

Compiled and edited by | JANE MAGRATH

Alfred

Preface

Some of the most rewarding keyboard music for progressing performers is the sonatina literature. Pianists for many years have been drawn to the Clementi *Sonatinas, Op. 36* and to many of those by Kuhlau. *Sonatina Masterworks* Book 2 includes the familiar Clementi *Sonatina in G Major, Op. 36, No. 2* and the Beethoven *Sonatinas in G and F Major.* The additional works in Book 2 also continue to develop skills needed to play some of the more difficult works from the standard sonatina literature as well as other well-known Clementi sonatinas. This book and Book 3 contain both familiar and well-loved sonatinas as well as several less well-known works of high quality.

The works are included in their entirety. The Kabalevsky sonatina is complete in one movement, and others are two-movement works. Dynamic indications, phrase markings and fingerings are editorial. Every effort has been made to retain the highest standard in stylistic articulation and overall performance, while encouraging basic musicality and taking advantage of the capabilities of the modern instrument.

Included in each book is a chart showing a possible order for repertoire study, with pieces listed by individual sonatina movement. Movements of individual sonatinas sometimes vary in difficulty. Some students will complete entire sonatinas, while others may study selected movements from throughout the volume.

Performer's Corner notes for the student are presented at the end of each book. This section contains quick hints to help make these pieces easier to learn and perform. The objective was to isolate one or two central points in each piece to begin the learning process.

I extend warm thanks and sincere appreciation to Morty and Iris Manus and to E. L. Lancaster for their vision, support and help with these volumes.

A Special Note for the Performer

These pieces have been selected with you, the performer, in mind. Every attempt has been made to provide music of the highest quality that will be appealing to you and your audiences. Best wishes for many hours of delight, joy and beauty as you practice and perform these selections. Most importantly, listen carefully to your playing as you practice, and enjoy every piece that you read or study!

Jane Magrath

Suggested Progressive Order for Study

Works are approximately equal in difficulty within a group and are listed alphabetically. Selections in Group A are the least difficult.

GROUP A

Beethoven . . . .*1st movement from Sonatina in G*
Köhler . . . .*1st movement*
Latour . . . .*1st movement*
Latour . . . .*2nd movement*
Lynes . . . .*1st movement*
Lynes . . . .*2nd movement*
Pleyel . . . .*1st movement*
Spindler . . . .*1st movement*
Spindler . . . .*2nd movement*

GROUP B

Beethoven . . . .*1st movement from Sonatina in F*
Beethoven . . . . . .*2nd movement from Sonatina in G*
Clementi . . . .*2nd movement*
Clementi . . . .*3rd movement*
Köhler . . . .*2nd movement*
Köhler . . . .*3rd movement*
Latour . . . .*3rd movement*
Lynes . . . .*3rd movement*
Pleyel . . . .*2nd movement*
Schmitt . . . .*1st movement*

GROUP C

Beethoven . . . .*2nd movement from Sonatina in F*
Clementi . . . .*1st movement*
Kabalevsky . . . .*Sonatina in A Minor*
Kuhlau . . . .*1st movement*
Kuhlau . . . .*2nd movement*
Schmitt . . . .*2nd movement*

LITERATURE LEVELS
for Sonatina Masterworks, Books 1–3

based on
The Pianist's Guide to Standard Teaching and Performance Literature
by Jane Magrath

Book covers are placed to show approximate grading of each volume based on the Level chart from *The Pianist's Guide to Standard Teaching and Performance Literature.*

Level 1   Bartók *Mikrokosmos, Volume 1*

Level 2   Türk *Pieces for Beginners*

Level 3   Latour *Sonatinas*
             Kabalevsky *Pieces for Young People, Op. 39*

Level 4   *Anna Magdalena Bach Notebook*
             Gurlitt *Album for the Young, Op. 140*
             Tchaikovsky *Album for the Young, Op. 39*

Level 5   *Anna Magdalena Bach Notebook*
             Attwood, Lynes *Sonatinas*
             Menotti *Poemetti*

Level 6   Clementi *Sonatinas, Op. 36*
             Burgmüller *25 Progressive Pieces, Op. 100*

Level 7   Kuhlau and moderate Diabelli *Sonatinas*
             Bach easiest *Two-Part Inventions*
             Bach *Short Preludes*
             Dello Joio *Lyric Pieces for the Young*

Level 8   Bach moderately difficult *Two-Part Inventions*
             Beethoven easiest variation sets
             Field *Nocturnes*
             Schumann *Album Leaves, Op. 124*
             Schubert *Waltzes*
             Turina *Miniatures*

Level 9   Bach *Two-Part Inventions*
             Haydn easiest sonata movements
             Mendelssohn easiest *Songs Without Words*
             Chopin easiest *Mazurkas*

Level 10   Bach easiest *Three-Part Inventions*
             Chopin easiest *Nocturnes*
             Beethoven *Sonatas, Op. 49, 79*
             Mozart *Sonata, K. 283*
             Muczynski *Preludes*

Sonatina in G Major
I.

Louis Köhler
(1820–1886)

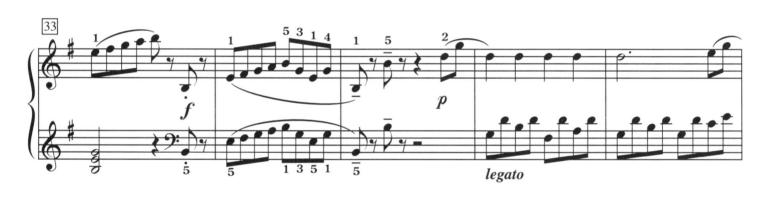

II.

ⓐ Play the ornaments quickly on the beat.

III.

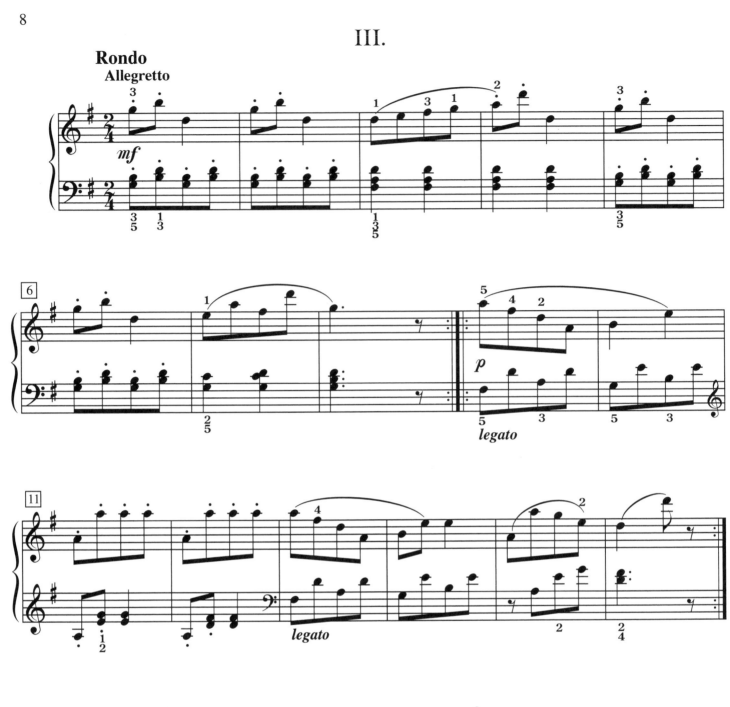

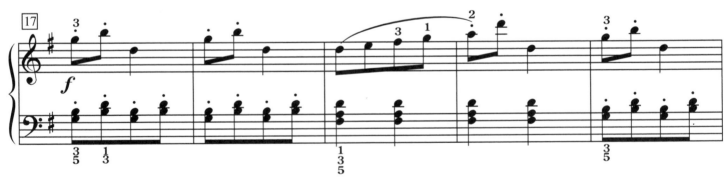

Sonatina in C Major
Op. 157, No. 1
I.

Fritz Spindler
(1817–1905)

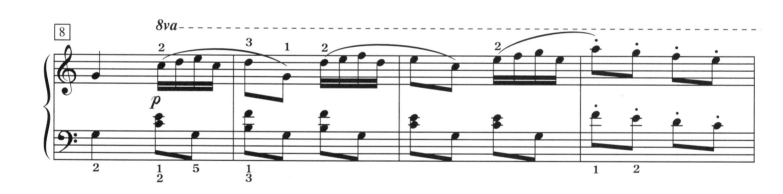

II.

Tarantella
Vivace

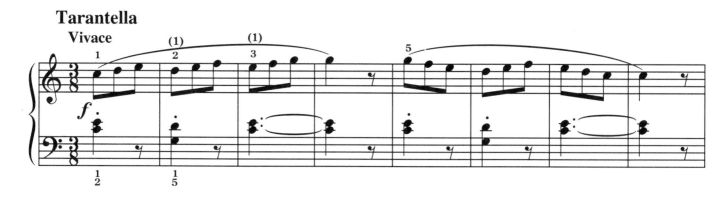

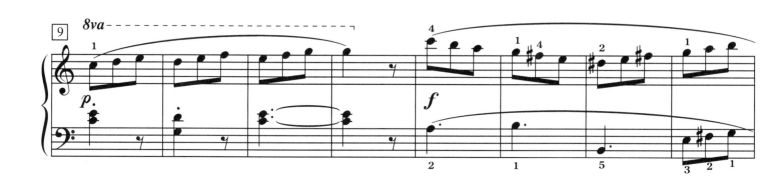

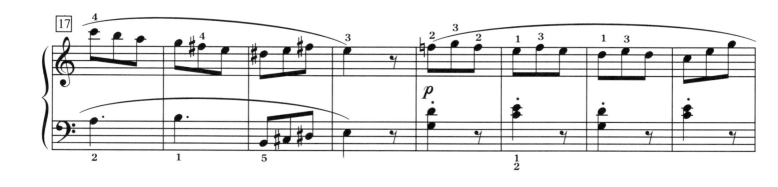

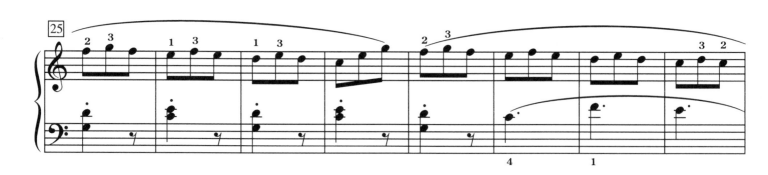

Sonatina No. 2 in G Major
I.

Theodore Latour
(1766–1837)

II.

III.

Tema con variazioni

Moderato

Variation II

Sonatina in G Major

Anh. 5, No. 1

I.

Ludwig van Beethoven
(1770–1827)

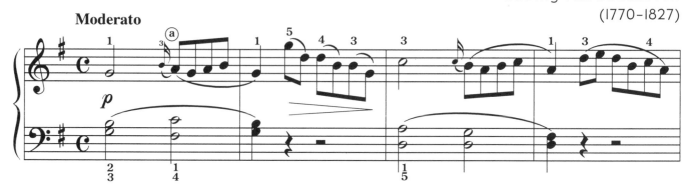

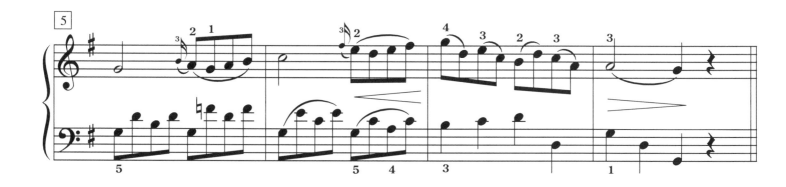

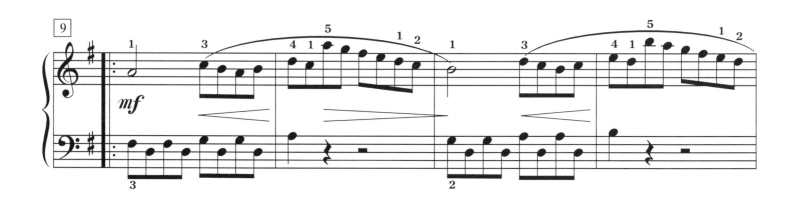

ⓐ Appogiaturas may be played either on the beat as sixteenth notes or very quickly before the beat.

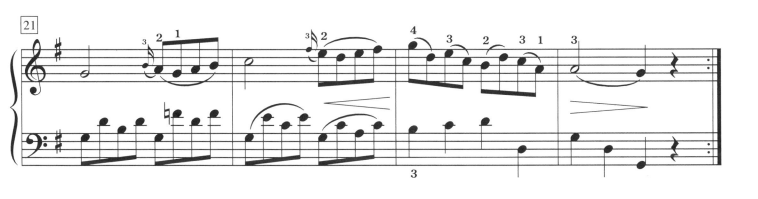

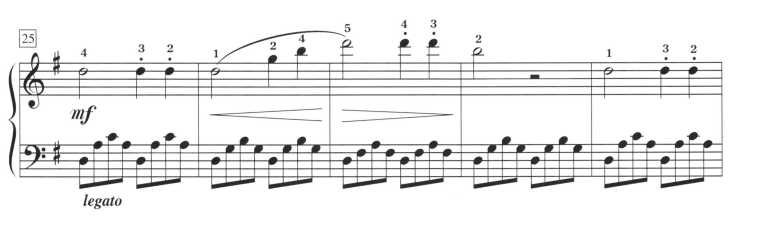

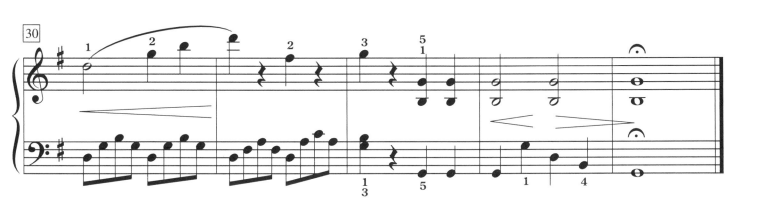

II.

Sonatina in F Major

Anh. 5, No. 2

I.

Ludwig van Beethoven
(1770-1827)

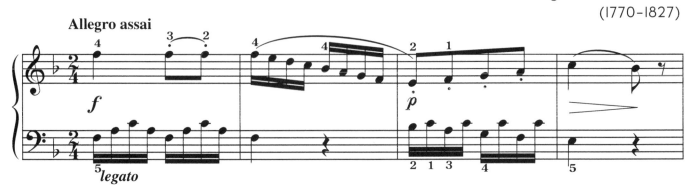

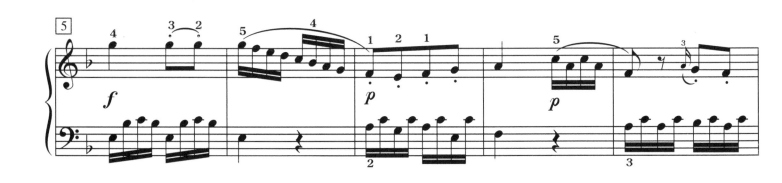

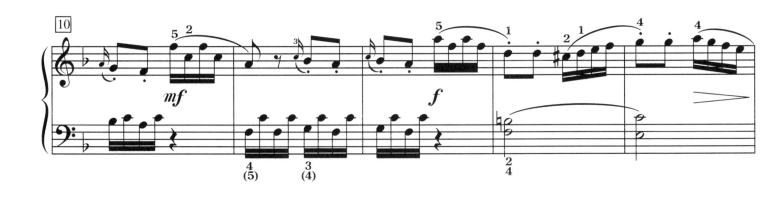

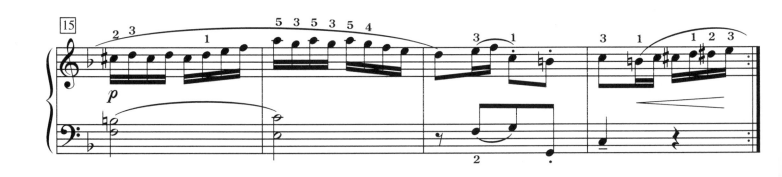

II.

Rondo
Allegro

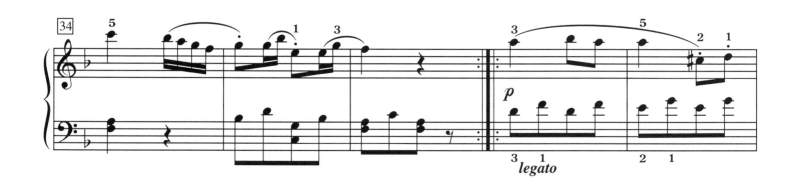

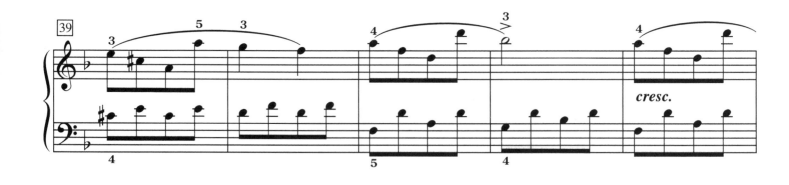

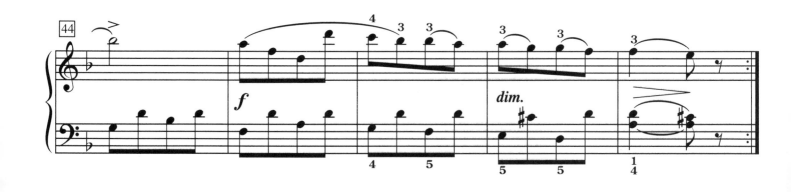

Sonatina in C Major
Op. 39, No. 1
I.

Frank Lynes
(1858–1913)

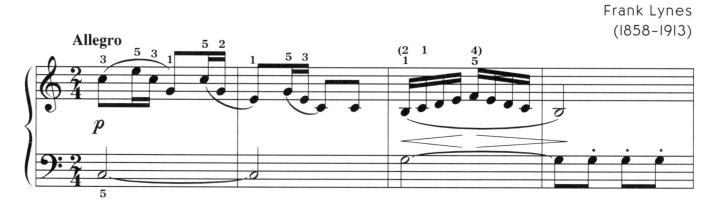

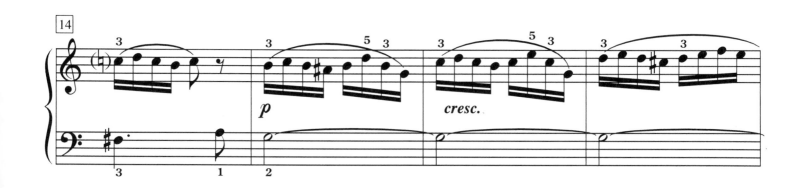

II.

Minuet
Allegretto

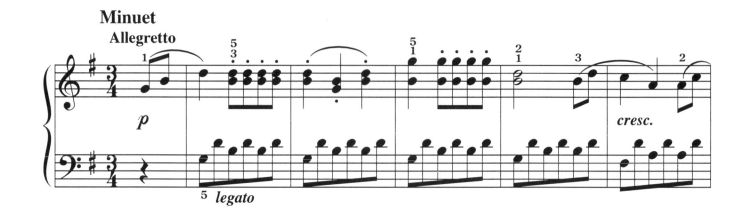

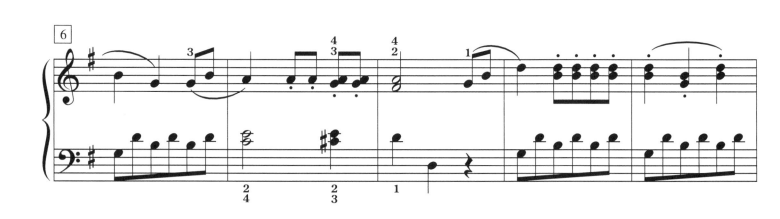

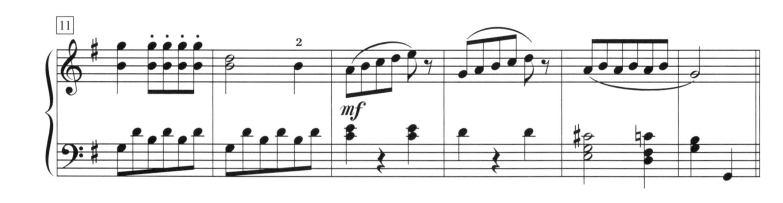

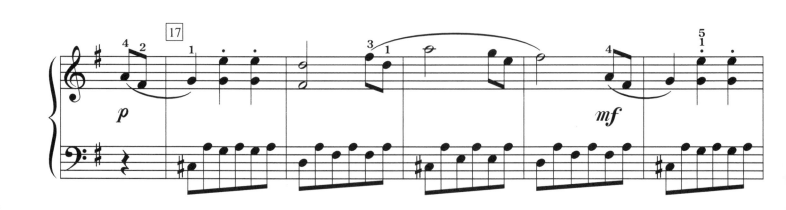

III.

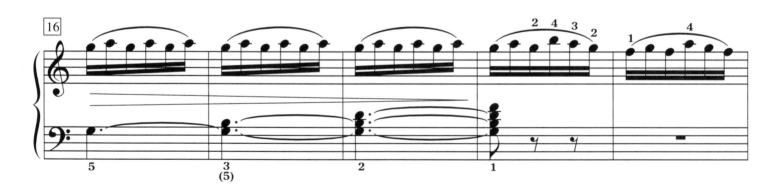

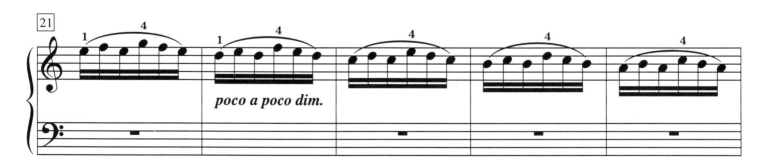

Sonatina in C Major
I.

Ignaz Joseph Pleyel
(1757–1831)

II.

Rondo
Poco allegretto

Sonatina in A Minor
Op. 27, No. 18

Dmitri Kabalevsky
(1904–1987)

Sonatina in C Major

I.

Jacob Schmitt
(1803–1853)

II.

ⓐ Play ornaments as crushed notes, quickly on the beat.

Sonatina in G Major

Op. 36, No. 2

I.

Muzio Clementi
(1752–1832)

II.

III.

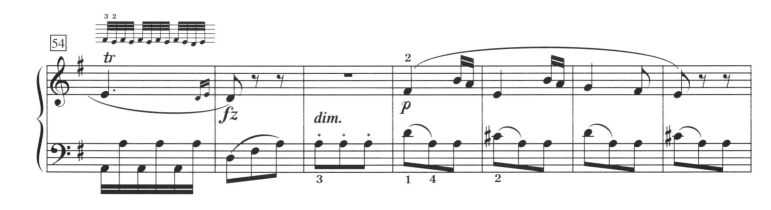

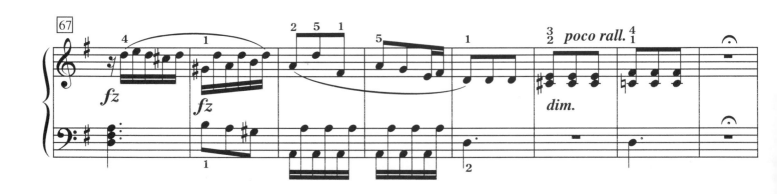

Sonatina in C Major
Op. 55, No. 1

I.

Friedrich Kuhlau
(1786–1832)

II.

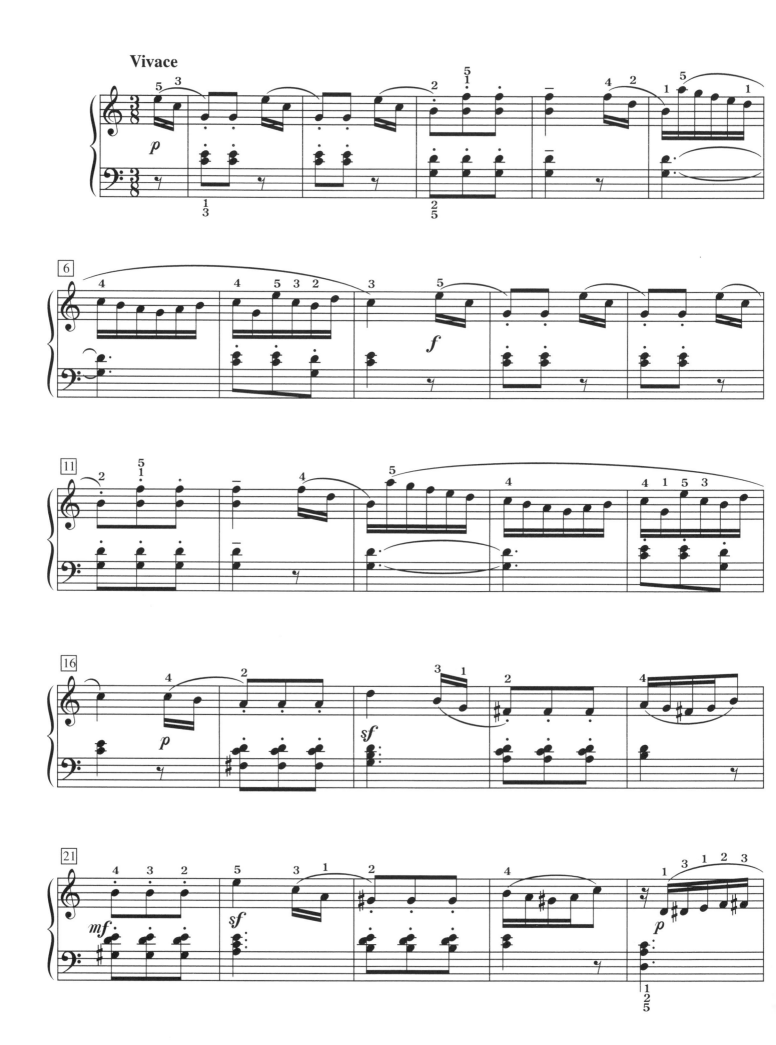

THE PERFORMER'S CORNER

Quick hints to help make these pieces easier to learn and perform.

Köhler, Louis *Sonatina in G Major* 5

I.   Allegro moderato
- Identify as many different triads, inversions and other chords as possible in this movement.

II.   Andante cantabile
- This movement consists of four sections: A B A′ Codetta. Mark the sections in your music.

III. Rondo—Allegretto
- The music changes from major to minor in measure 25. Name the minor key.

Spindler, Fritz *Sonatina in C Major, Op. 157, No. 1* 10

I.   Allegro
- The opening six-note right-hand motive (♩♫♩ ♩ ♩) is found throughout the movement. How many measures do *not* contain this motive?

II.   Tarantella—Vivace
- What elements can add excitement to the performance after the fermata in measure 62?
- Perform this piece with one pulse for every measure.
- This movement is a dance. Would you describe it as a moderate dance similar to a waltz, or as a lively dance that is almost frantic?

Latour, Theodore *Sonatina No. 2 in G Major* 14

I.   Allegretto
- This movement consists of four sections. Here the final A section is varied slightly from the beginning, and the form is A B A′ Codetta. Mark the sections in your music.
- How does Latour vary the A′ section from the opening A section? Compare measures 5–8 with measures 24–27. Circle the first measure in the last section that varies from the first section.

II.   Andante
- The melody in this movement needs to sing above the accompaniment. What are some ways to play with a true legato and a smooth, seamless sound?

III. Tema con variazioni—Moderato
- Experiment by playing the staccatos in the first measure of the theme and in the variations in several different ways. Listen to hear how the length of the staccato notes and the touch used in playing staccatos can affect the mood.
- Determine a mood(s) that you want to portray for each variation. Practice setting the mood for the theme and variations by playing the first four measures of each, one after another.

Beethoven, Ludwig van *Sonatina in G Major, Anh. 5, No. 1* .18

I. Moderato
- The short slurs in measures 2, 7 and similar places indicate that the music needs inflection at this point, just as the human voice inflects as one speaks. Find other measures similar to these.
- The form of this piece is A B A Codetta. Which of these four sections is the longest? Mark the sections in your music.

II. Romanze — Moderato
- This work consists of four sections: A B A Codetta. Mark the sections in your music.

Beethoven, Ludwig van *Sonatina in F Major, Anh. 5, No. 2* .22

I. Allegro assai
- Compare measures 1–8 with measures 19–26. How does Beethoven vary these measures to create surprise?

II. Rondo — Allegro
- The main theme returns several times in *rondo* form, alternating with other themes in between. Write A in your music the two times that the main A theme (meas. 1–16) or a shortened version of it returns.

Lynes, Frank *Sonatina in C Major, Op. 39, No. 1* 28

I. Allegro
- This sonatina movement is filled with broken chords and inversions. Circle all of the broken chords in this movement.
- A long sequence appears in measures 9–14. Name the beginning and ending notes of this sequential passage. Use the sequential ideas to aid in memorizing the RH alone in this section.

II. Minuet — Allegro
- The three sections of the A B A form in this piece begin in measures 1, 16 and 32. Mark the three sections in your music.

III. Allegro
- As in the first movement, a long sequence appears in measures 19–25. Name the beginning and ending notes of the sequential passage. Play the sequence by memory.
- How will you end the sequential passage in measure 26 to make a smooth transition back to the main theme in measure 27?

Pleyel, Ignaz Joseph *Sonatina in C Major* 34

I. Tempo di minuetto
- In *minuet and trio* form, such as this movement, the performer must take the repeats in the A and B section, but not take the repeat when the A section returns. In this movement you will play the sections as follows: A (a a b b) B (c c d d) A (a b).

II. Rondo — Poco allegretto
- Some of the music in this movement is quite humorous and designed to surprise the listener. How can you achieve this humor in measures 31–34?

Kabalevsky, Dmitri *Sonatina in A minor, Op. 27, No. 18* 36

- Circle each descending broken triad in this piece.
  Practice the broken chords using the appropriate fingering.
- Circle each ascending or descending scale passage in this piece.
  Some scale passages use fingers 1 2 3 only; others use 1 2 3 4 only.
  Do any use a combination of 1 2 3 and 1 2 3 4?

Schmitt, Jacob *Sonatina in C Major* 38

I.   Moderato
- The different left hand legato and staccato sections should assist you
  in varying the mood between the different themes in this piece.

II. Rondo—Allegretto
- This work has four sections: A B A′ Codetta. Mark the sections in your music.
  Notice that the A sections are in the key of C while the B section begins in the key of G.

Clementi, Muzio *Sonatina in G Major, Op. 36, No. 2* 42

I.   Allegretto
- This movement is in sonata-allegro form, a common form for first movements in
  sonatas. The themes in the *exposition* or opening section, measures 1–22, are
  presented in contrasting keys, G and D. Notice that the themes in the last section
  of sonata-allegro form, the *recapitulation*, measures 36–59, are the same but both
  are in the key of G. The middle section of sonata-allegro movements, the *development*,
  found here in measures 22–36, is where the themes may be presented in new keys
  or developed.

II. Allegretto
- Circle the beats in this movement that do not have the lilting rhythm (♩. ♪)
  in the right or left hand. Notice that these beats are only at cadences.
- Mark the A B A sections in your music.

III. Allegro
- The contrasting ideas in this movement should be played with a different character
  or mood for each. Write an adjective in the music to describe the different moods
  of the themes beginning at measures 1, 32, 41, 49 and 57.

Kuhlau, Friedrich *Sonatina in C Major, Op. 55, No. 1* 48

I.   Allegro
- This movement is in sonata-allegro form, similar to the first movement of the Clementi
  Sonatina in G, Op. 36, No. 2. Mark the three sections (exposition, development and
  recapitulation) in your music. Compare the theme in measures 9–20 to that in
  measures 51–62. How are they similar? How are they different?

II. Vivace
- This movement is in rondo form. Mark the A theme each time it recurs in this
  movement. How many times does the A theme appear? Which time is it varied?